The Adjacent K

THOMAS BLACKBURN

The Adjacent Kingdom
COLLECTED LAST POEMS

Edited and with an Introduction by
Jean MacVean

PETER OWEN · LONDON

ISBN 0 7206 0707 8

PETER OWEN PUBLISHERS
73 Kenway Road London SW5 0RE

Poems © The Thomas Blackburn Estate 1980
Foreword and Introduction © Peter Owen Ltd 1988

Photoset in Great Britain by Photosetting Yeovil Somerset
Printed by Antony Rowe Ltd Chippenham Wilts

In memory of Margaret Blackburn

To show just how movement is when we are dead,
I mean with an uncircumscribed freedom
In that meaningful and adjacent kingdom
Which by the climbing of rock is suggested.

Thomas Blackburn

We climbed, he first, I following, till to sight
    Appeared those things of beauty that heaven wears
    Glimpsed through a rounded opening, faintly bright,
Thence issuing, we beheld again the stars.

Dante, *The Inferno* (trans. Laurence Binyon)

FOREWORD

It was towards the end of the Second World War that
Tambimuttu, Editor of *Poetry London*, brought Thomas Blackburn
to visit me – an astonishingly handsome, but sensitively nervous
young man, who took me aback by asking me point-blank, 'and
will you not mind being put in a hole, and earth shovelled over
your face?' Already death was a theme that at once horrified and
attracted him. At that time my own concern with death was small
and if anything theoretical. I might have replied by quoting Plato
or Plotinus. But Blackburn's confrontation had little regard for
theories or the 'history of ideas': he was from the outset committed
to living the life of his soul, that 'pilgrim of eternity'.

Yeats somewhere objects that whereas theologians discuss first
causes and final ends, we should above all like to know where we
were a little before birth, and where we shall be a little after death;
hence Yeats's studies in psychical research, and also Blackburn's
lifelong interest in these matters. His most important work of
criticism is his book on Robert Browning; he too was concerned to
know what awaits us beyond death. There is more than a trace of
Browning's influence on Blackburn's style – or perhaps rather a
natural affinity. A friend for many years was Wilson Knight. To
none of those named did any form of materialism carry the
slightest conviction. For Blackburn himself his journey of life was
a hard one, but few poets have found at the close a certainty more
radiant of an ultimate beatitude. This collection is more than
another volume of good poems – it bears witness (as poets should)
to the deep mystery of life.

C. G. Jung wrote of the importance of 'thinking our thoughts to
the end'. Not many people have possessed the capacity to the
extent to which Thomas Blackburn was prepared to carry this
heroic exercise – hence much of that suffering which most of us
avoid by stopping short. Jung speaks of 'thinking our thoughts', but
for Blackburn it was above all the life of feeling that he explored
with such unflinching honesty. Few have suffered more in this
naked confrontation, and had his death come earlier it could have

found him in despair. This was not to be: our last discussions were far different from that first one. Not by conviction or by 'faith', but by visionary insight Thomas Blackburn *knew* that 'the steep ascent' (he was himself a mountaineer) leads indeed to

> That sweet golden clime
> Where the traveller's journey is done.

During his last years – indeed his last months – he wrote poems, and wonderful letters, telling of what he had experienced. The last letter I received I read in ignorance that he had already died when I was reading it. It must have been one of the last he wrote, and he spoke of his joyful anticipation of returning to his cottage in Wales where he would see 'the unskinned stars'. This phrase he uses in some of his last poems also. His soul had already become 'unskinned' some time before, but, happily for us, he was permitted to return to this world for long enough to tell us something of what he knew.

His was not one of those 'courageous' deaths of sufferers from some grim disease, who endure patiently and testify to human fortitude – indeed he was hardly ill in this sense at all. He was rather a gnostic than a stoic of death, and he wrote of the 'end-stopped' character of poets unwilling or unable to discern the meaning of the soul's journey.

The other side of soul's experience in this world is love; which Blackburn gave and received abundantly, in both his first and his second marriages. He loved his daughter Julia, he loved his friends. Drunk he often was, and too startlingly, truthfully outspoken for the liking of those less committed than he was himself to a life of unswerving integrity. Yet it is that very quality which was to ensure not only his own final illumination, but that his poems live on.

Kathleen Raine

CONTENTS

Acknowledgements 10
Introduction 11

January 1975　23
Resurge　24
December　25
Exodus　26
Conversation Piece　27
Alcoholism　28
Zennor　29
Schizophrenia　30
Maturation　31
My Wife　32
Halloo　33
Supper　34
Daughter　35
Legion　36
Companion　37
My Daughter Julia　38
Insomnia　39
All Change　40
Lent　41
Knowing　42
Domine　43
Vernal　44
The Pearl　45
A Salutation　46
Morituri (1)　47
Unpredictable　48
College　49
Being Alone　51
Common Sense　52
Blame　53
Senex　54
A Visit　56
Nadir　57
Brynhyfryd (1)　58

Retirement　59
For Margaret　60
Casa Montini　61
Home　62
Clinical Depression　63
Mountain　64
Sorrow　65
Crib-y-Dysgil　66
Headlined Review　68
Jubilate　69
There　70
Laudate　71
Moel Wnion　72
The Raven　73
Posthumous　74
Pathways　75
Morituri (2)　76
Dualities　78
Steel　79
Sober　80
Dauphiné　81
Nobis Pacem　82
Meeting　83
Speed　84
Ageing　85
Mid-October　86
To Be Continued　87
Never the Less　88
Pre-Natal　89
Choosing　90
Brynhyfryd (2)　91
With You　93
Purgatorial　94

ACKNOWLEDGEMENTS

I should like to record my appreciation to the late Margaret Blackburn for generously handing the poems to me to edit, Julia Bonger (née Blackburn) for her help as Executor and Mrs Rosalie Blackburn for useful information and good wishes.

I should also like to thank Professor Roger Sharrock, Dr A.A. Evans and William Cookson for valuable advice and suggestions; and Kathleen Raine, John Heath-Stubbs and Lettice Cooper for their benign interest.

Finally, I wish to thank the Brotherton Library, University of Leeds, as well as Durham University, for their generous support.

Some of the poems in this collection have previously appeared in the following publications: *Agenda*, *Aquarius*, *Chronicles* (USA), *Interim* (USA), *The Listener*, *P.E.N. Broadsheet*, *PN Review*, *Poetry Nation*, *Poetry Review*, *The Tablet* and *Temenos*.

J.M.

INTRODUCTION

Thomas Eliel Fenwick Blackburn was born at Hensingham in Cumbria on 10 February 1916. The fact that he was given his father's Christian and his mother's maiden names, though a convention of the times, serves to underline the deep involvement with his parents which was a prime cause of later emotional difficulties. This conflict was barely resolved before his death in Wales in August 1977 at the age of sixty-one. Indeed they were the last people he saw. 'It seemed that Eliel and Adelaide – though my hair prickled at the prospect – were here.'[1]

Eliel Blackburn, a clergyman, had been brought up in Mauritius, where his family had moved in the early days of British rule. He was obsessed by the idea that there might be 'colour' in the family and by a nervous distrust of sexuality. Emphasised by somewhat savage ideas of discipline, he projected these obsessions on to his son. The relationship between the parents, too, was uneasy and Blackburn developed an Oedipal attachment to his mother. She provided him with another problem: her refusal to consider any question that might be deemed contentious or disturbing. Also Blackburn believed that his later alcoholism was in part caused by the fact that she had insisted on feeding him herself when suffering from a breast abscess.

He dealt with his early life in a picaresque autobiography, *A Clip of Steel*, and in an interesting early poem, 'Family History'.

> She looked at him; he bowed his head;
> They nodded and between them both
> Stepped down into that childish bed
> The shadow of their undergrowth.
> So that which they refused to bear
> Or suffer, and had thrust apart,
> Became the colour of his hair
> And substance of his beating heart.

In this poem it is clear that Blackburn believed that the unsolved problems of his parents inevitably became part of his own structure, a 'terrible heritage'.

Eliel Blackburn was well liked and respected by his parishioners and it is impossible to know precisely what so distorted the situation between father and son. It is, however, certain that the relationship darkened Blackburn's life and that he devoted much of his time and intelligence to trying to come to terms with it. To the end, he seems to have seen his father with the terror of a frightened child. 'How could he help the astigmatism of his dreadful eyes?'[2]

The emotional disturbance may, of course, have been caused by an unavoidable incompatibility. Perhaps the child was simply overwhelmed by a disturbingly powerful personality. 'Every human body', writes Elmire Zolla, 'is a construction with a peculiar magnetic field of its own, its psyche. The approach of a stronger field of energy can be devastating: the psyche is necessarily moved and changed, sometimes it ceases to exist under the impact.'[3]

One of the routes of escape is through a descent into the interior world. 'For the poet,' Blackburn wrote, 'this journey is necessary, since it is within the darkness of himself that he confronts the powers of the imagination.'[4] He believed that

> ... the poet has the double vision of the god Odin; with his blinded eye he beholds what is going on in the night of himself; his other eye watches the outer scene. If one of his eyes is not blind then he becomes, at best, just a clever reporter of external phenomena; on the other hand if both are blind, he is lost in the shadows. Given this double vision of light and dark, he is able to inter-relate the two worlds and interpret them to each other.[5]

Blackburn was of course, brought up in a religious household and although he rejected orthodoxy ('I never pray except in the sense of writing poetry'),[6] his attitude was that of the religious poet of his time, deeply affected by the psychological discoveries of Freud and Jung and forced therefore to attempt to come to terms with the inner heaven and hell. 'Today it is the inward significance which matters, as if the gods had shifted their centre of gravity from the external plane to the inner kingdom of ourselves.'[7]

Blackburn, as Dr A.A. Evans, formerly principal of the College of St Mark and St John, perceived, had a 'curious kind of God-haunted charisma.... Underneath there were dark things to be satisfied – or satiated.'[8]

Blackburn's openness and a peculiar transparency, as well as the fact that he refused to take refuge in comforting illusions, brought the light and the dark very near the surface. The one-eyed monsters of 'Halloo' were always waiting for an opening; but so, too, was Apollo, the power of poetry, 'that supreme exorcist',[9] who had turned and confronted the Furies in open court, thus mitigating and halting the murderous destiny of the House of Atreus.

At his father's wish, Blackburn studied law at Cambridge after being educated at a minor public school. He discovered drink as a means of freeing and enlarging the perceptions and of dissolving his self-consciousness. It lifted the burden of guilt which oppressed him and returned him to the peculiar clarity of childhood. More important, it altered his vision. He saw the evening shadows, the bottles of a saloon bar with a painter's eye, while a nearby river 'achieved a dark and glittering majesty'.[10] He began, somewhat dangerously, to believe that this heightened vision, though founded on the use of alcohol, was nearer the reality he sought than that of the sober everyday.

He was sent down from Cambridge after a minor misdemeanour and had a breakdown which led him to psychoanalysis. During his treatment, he took a room at a London hotel and tried to penetrate some of the meanings of existence, reading Schopenhauer, Bergson, Blake, Plato and Nietzsche 'as if my life depended on it'.[11]

He recovered sufficiently to take a degree in English at Durham University (as he had always wanted) in 1940. He also married Joan Arnold, a fellow-student, but this relationship was short-lived. He was a pacifist during the war and therefore given somewhat unpleasant war work, first as coal-trimmer in a Polish merchant navy trading vessel, then in the London Stretcher Party and finally in the National Fire Service. In 1945, after his divorce, he married the painter Rosalie de Méric. His daughter Julia, to whom he was devoted, was born in 1948. During his time at Durham he had discovered what was to become an absorbing passion: rock climbing. He made many climbs with his wife and introduced the great British mountaineer Chris Bonington to the sport. As he grew older, he came to see climbing as 'a metaphor . . . For the way we move from time to the eternities'.[12]

His marriage, at first happy, lasted for twenty years and ended in divorce. In 1963 he married Margaret Gerhardis, who 'made, at least this wanderer, a strong home/From a promiscuous, vagrant vacancy'.[13] He dedicated three volumes of his verse to Rosalie de Méric and wrote several poems referring to their climbs together ('Senex' and 'Dauphiné' in the present collection). Those to his widow are some of his finest and chart the deepening strength of their relationship.

After the war, Blackburn spent twelve years teaching, principally at Marylebone Grammar School. He was later a lecturer at the College of St Mark and St John, Chelsea, and, finally, at Whitelands College, Putney, retiring at sixty. 'He was a brilliant teacher, successful indeed in examination results, but also lighting a fire in many students, both in class, and in other things, such as poetry readings, bringing creative people to College and talking to some of his students until late at night in his home at Putney or in his Welsh cottage.'[14] One of his ex-students, Philip Boothby, found

> . . . his lectures stimulating and challenging. Within minutes of starting, he would be ranging brilliantly over topics seemingly only tenuously connected with his main theme. Each and every student would be brought into the discussion. There could be no 'passengers'. He would lean forward, his jaw jutting aggressively, finishing a question with his often-impersonated interrogative grunt. And such was the force of his patent enthusiasm and commitment that an answer – even if not always immediately on target – was always forthcoming. He taught us not only to love literature more deeply, but also to think and question: to be honest in our responses; to respect a text. He had no time for pretentiousness or insincerity in our written work, or in us as people. He gave such things very short shrift.[15]

It was during the fifties that Blackburn began to make his reputation as a poet. He published four volumes of verse, much of it influenced by Yeats, whom he admired as 'always concerned with those manifestations of life where we are overshadowed by powers which are vastly more than our everyday selves, where the curtains of platitude and convention are lifted for a moment and there is a glimpse of the great strangeness of our destiny'.[16] This strangeness, for Blackburn, was intimately connected with the idea of death. 'For death, when all is said and done, is the direction of life, and just as in the womb the foetus must grow organs which are appropriate for this world, so here we must grow spiritually if we are to be ready for the kingdom of death. Such growth is the chief aim of human endeavour.'[17] The meaning of death was throughout his life an urgent concern. He could be said, as was said of the Celts, to have practised the Craft of Dying.

His first poem was published in *Adam*, still edited by Miron Grindea today. Another in *The Glass* led him to Erica Marx of the Hand and Flower Press who published his first small collection. At that time, Blackburn was too diffident to submit work to magazines or publishers and the poems were typed and sent out by his wife, who suppressed any rejections. His early poems included work on mythological themes: 'Orpheus', 'Orpheus and Eurydice', 'Bacchae', 'Pasiphae' and 'Cnossus'. As he matured, however, he moved away from the influence of Yeats and from myth and legend towards his own individual voice and experience. He said in an interview: 'It was only when there were certain things that I wanted to say that Yeats hadn't said that I began seriously to want to write.' Edward Lucie-Smith considered that Blackburn's most original poems offered 'a bleak geography of the domestic emotions which is in fact quite different from anything to be found in Yeats or in the Movement poets who sometimes use the same material'.[18] Blackburn was becoming known in the period after Dylan Thomas's death when the Movement poets were taking their stand against modernism and internationalism. He was, as Roy Fuller said, 'a relentless and probing critic of his own psyche'. These investigations were not a narrow preoccupation, but rather attempts to understand man, his problems and his destiny.

The poet's vision restores to us some inkling of what we really are, and suggests the mystery of human nature, shading off as it does into energies, heights and depths which are beyond the scope of our workaday intellect. . . . Because poetry enables us to glimpse this other dimension, it restores man and Nature to their proper majesty and significance.[19]

The poems were passionate, disciplined, technically accomplished and followed traditional verse patterns. One of Blackburn's strengths was his ability to speak with unmasked sincerity using an interesting, very individual vocabulary.

Blackburn was Gregory Fellow at Leeds in 1956 and 1957. His radio play, *A Place of Meeting*, was performed on the BBC Third Programme in 1956. In 1960 his poem 'The Sediment' won the principal Guinness Award. *A Breathing Space* (1964) was a Poetry Book Society Recommendation. *The Judas Tree*, a musical drama with music by Peter Dickinson, was first produced in 1965. An interpretation in contemporary music and verse of some aspects of Christianity, it dealt with the problem of evil. It was later performed at the cathedrals in Edinburgh, Liverpool, Southwark and Washington, DC. *The Times* considered it 'the most compelling and deeply considered religious work since Britten's *War Requiem*'.

In all, Blackburn published twelve collections of poetry, one volume of verse translations (with others), five anthologies, three volumes of criticism and a novel, *Feast for the Wolf* (1971). His autobiography, *A Clip of Steel*, was published in 1969. He was a Fellow of the Royal Society of Literature.

His own experiences led him to consider the problem of suffering. One of his most often anthologised poems is 'Hospital for Defectives' with its final question:

> Lord of the Images, whose love
> The eyelid and the rose
> Takes for a metaphor, today
> Beneath the warder's blows
> The unleavened man did not cry out
> Or turn his face away;
> Through such men in a turnip field
> What is it that you say?

Selected Poems, a distillation of the best of Blackburn's work to that date, was published in 1975, while *Post Mortem* (1977) gained its title because he believed, as a result of a visionary experience in his Welsh cottage, that 'my first dying occurred/On a Monday in July'. His posthumously published *Bread for the Winter Birds* (1980) reveals aspects of his new vision:

> Have you ever had moments when the curtain lifted
> And showed you deeper ways of how to see
> As if away the mist on creatures drifted
> And fixed them with a new intensity?[20]

His influences were Browning, Wordsworth, Blake, Eliot and Hopkins. Keats persisted under the surface. The poems, less regular as Blackburn grew older, were those of a man gnarled and scarred by experience.

> I am, as Blake said, the secretary of the word
> And to get words down with an extreme accuracy,
> Have ravaged myself almost to excess and with brutality.[21]

The work in the present collection was written during his last few years. The poems are in approximately chronological order, opening with reflections on his breakdown in the early seventies and subsequent time in hospital. Appalling though this experience must have been, it appeared to clear his screen for the visionary experience which came later. This experience, of which he wrote in *Light*, the journal of the College of Psychic Studies, profoundly affected the rest of his life. It took place in his Welsh cottage, starting as

> ... a dream of exceptional intensity and then continued as a vision, half spoken to my inward ear by an invisible chronicler, half projected in coloured images on the whitewashed walls.
>   In the dream I was dying and for a few moments felt an extreme terror, sensing an invisible hand feeling for certain nerves in the region of my throat ... I felt the fingers undoing a ganglion, almost a knot of nerves. The knot came free, there was a click, and my next impression was one of blinding light

particularly associated with lilies, and irises of blue and red, although the whole was of an intense gold I have only seen on some dawn in the Italian dolomites. . . . I saw a silver garment suitable for either male or female, and if it fitted me, understood I would have achieved a certain wholeness, in that I would have come into communion with the female component of my soul. . . . I was told that I would soon return.

Blackburn believed that during this experience he made the crossing from life into death. There was a prophetic meaning, but 'all I am certain of is the joy it has brought me and the sense that although I wish to live as long and as fully as possible, the process of dying is no longer a fear to me, but a source of considerable happiness'.[22]

The vision had not revealed the condition of death as black extinction but as a state of brilliant colour and intensity. Beside this, the words 'Rest in Peace' seemed absurd. It had not alarmed him; he had had paranormal experiences before and believed the Aquarian Age was about to make fresh discoveries in the field.

His nervous sensibility, alcoholism (which he had almost overcome before his death) and addiction to a psychiatric drug all damaged him. He was not happy at Whitelands College and was physically hampered, latterly, by a spinal injury. David Wright, who saw him two years before his death, later wrote: ' . . . I was shocked by his appearance. He looked ten years older than his real age, though still a remarkably handsome man: his face astonished me by its amazing and unexpected resemblance to Eliot's, as I had seen it a few months before Eliot's own death'. Nevertheless his ardent quest for meaning, from which he never deviated, did bring some of the certainties he sought, so that he lost his fear of death, and found illumination, both in the outside scene.

> Tonight through the leafage of a tree a single star.
> I saw it with eyes unskinned as perhaps it is,
> A mineral diagram of the numinous
> Glittering down from where the eternals are.[23]

and in close relationships:

I can be with you without speaking
And it is more satisfying than most speech,
And it is only with you that I have known the meaning of touching
And it is far beyond the circumstances of touch.[24]

In 'Pre-Natal' he wrote that, during the dreams and visionary experiences he continued to have until his death, he felt that he had been

> ... to where I was before I was born
> And in a quiet dialogue the self and I
> Decided upon my birthplace, a sufficiency
> Of evil in it and the child was to be torn
> By forces which, though terrible, I indeed chose
> For my own multifarious purposes.
> It was more possible to read the sentences
> In that black script and its wanton hammer-blows,
> And there, with the man I had chosen to call Father,
> To travel faster and much further.

In Plato's myth of Er, Er, slain in battle, is allowed to return as a messenger from the kingdom of the dead. He has seen souls 'awaiting the beginnings of another cycle of mortal generation' and finds they are free to choose their next incarnation and allowed to see the pattern of whatever life they select.

In 'Pre-Natal' Blackburn writes of his father:

> ... by subjecting me to his crooked regimen,
> Directing against me all that could abuse the soul,
> He speeded the process by which I could become serene and whole
> And in doing so succour dead women and dead men.
> For four decades he has been to me anathema,
> But though I castigate him in red letters,
> It was I myself who chose the thumbscrew and the fetters;
> For it was myself decided to go down there.

According to the myth, this choice is the supreme hazard for man, who must achieve enough wisdom in this life to enable him to select his next incarnation undazzled by the idea of wealth or the rewards of the tyrant. Er finally sees 'the new souls wafted upwards to their birth like shooting stars'.[25]

Blackburn died in the Welsh cottage where he had had his first vision. He is buried near the mountains he had often climbed. His wife was with him and wrote of his last days:

> He told me repeatedly that he was at last experiencing total earthly happiness. This newly reached serenity had come about through a fresh analysis with Dr Neil Micklem, begun earlier in the year through the advice of his friend Kathleen Raine. Thomas had derived great pleasure and confidence from this, saying that Neil Micklem was a true interpreter of Jung and could help him understand the strange, archetypal dreams which visited him from time to time. Dreams which often seemed more like visions. Through the doctor, he also found a way to accept the lifelong problem of his difficult and knotted relationship with his father.[26]

Despite Blackburn's extraordinary serenity, the atmosphere in the cottage was fateful. His wife was oppressed by a feeling of despondency and foreboding; and became aware of 'a long drawn out silence and the presence of a once living man who was not with me at all'. For the second time, Blackburn was moving into the new dimension, this time finally. On the last night 'at about two or three in the morning, there was a terrible cry'. When Margaret Blackburn reached him, Blackburn was already dead.

Towards the end of his life, he was deeply concerned with the idea of reconciliation. 'I see', he wrote in a letter to me, 'a whole new concept of forgiveness. You can only be free of your guilt if you forgive what Yeats calls "the mirror of malicious eyes":

> How in the name of heaven can he escape
> That defiling and disfigured shape
> The mirror of malicious eyes
> Casts upon his eye until at last
> He thinks that shape to be his shape?[27]

On the night he died he wrote to his brother, the writer John Blackburn, with whom he had quarrelled, a letter intended as a moving attempt at reconciliation. In the writing, however, it became the much more universal statement of a man in the last hours of life.

I have talked with my selfness, the godhead of my birth. It seemed that Eliel and Adelaide – though my hair prickled – were here. Recently I have in dreams met again the godhead and going recalled coming. I have heard the godhead speak as he spoke at first, desiring to be born into that by no means easy conjunction of Blackburn and Fenwick.

'So,' said the voice, 'you have indeed come through. I thought at times it might be intolerable, but now you have grown into the Thou of the Intention. Now you will grow here. No more will you need the iron maiden of carnality. Dear child, I have worked with you and you will grow here where the eternals are to further dyings and births, here in the dominion of the spirit.'

> Thou has delivered my soul from birth,
> My darling from the power of the dog.
> Natale, finite. Finite, natale.
> Pace. Pace. Pace.

... I have relived on the page the frightening and complete blackness, leading, supported by the Virgilian guide, through the hairy scrotum of the King of Darkness to rock, wan light, sun light, gloria.

... Now after hours of strange travel from dawn to dawn, though the mind burns, I must lie in a horizontal position and breathe long and deep.[28]

Professor Roger Sharrock has called this 'an extraordinary document which seems like looking out from the very edge of life and being able to say "in my end is my beginning"'.

Dr Evans has pointed out that the reference to Psalm 22 in the short poem, 'deliver my soul from the sword' has become 'Thou hast delivered my soul from birth'. In the Blackburn poem, therefore, the Psalmist's entreaty has been answered.

On a separate sheet in his last notebook, Blackburn wrote: 'The poet Kathleen Raine, friend and avatar, set my feet on the Dantesque descent or ascent, through the reaches of hell, the Devil's hairy genitalia, through and upwards to the starlit air and on to silence and unalcoholised energy to purgatory, and with Beatrice's occasional vista, I have glimpsed the celestial.'

Something of this journey may be found in the poems in this collection.

Jean MacVean

NOTES

1   Thomas Blackburn, Last Notebook.
2   'Pre-Natal'.
3   Elmire Zolla, *Archetypes*.
4   *The Price of an Eye* (1961).
5   Ibid.
6   *Light* (Winter 1974).
7   *The Price of an Eye*.
8   Dr A.A. Evans in a letter to me dated 11 January 1979.
9   Thomas Blackburn, *A Clip of Steel* (1969).
10 Ibid.
11 Ibid.
12 'Mountain'.
13 'Domine'.
14 Dr A.A. Evans in a letter to me dated 11 January 1979.
15 *College Year Book* (St Mark's and St John's, 1979).
16 *The Price of an Eye*.
17 Ibid.
18 *British Poetry since 1945*, ed. Edward Lucie-Smith (1970).
19 *The Price of an Eye*.
20 'At Dawn', op. cit.
21 'Nobis Pacem'.
22 *Light* (Winter 1974).
23 'Purgatorial'.
24 'With You'.
25 Plato, *The Republic*.
26 Foreword to *Bread for the Winter Birds* (1980).
27 Yeats, 'A Dialogue of Self and Soul'.
28 Last Notebook.

JANUARY 1975

Time to remember
With no regret
Now the year's turned over,
Seventy-four's start,
Bursting into madness
From the inchoate heart.

And now this living
Upon any sea,
Novelties of giving,
Serenity.

And the utter blackness
Which had to be
For sanity, dying,
Which I don't fear,
Though avid for seeing.

So that when no more
I can be found,
I'll leave my friends here
A piece of mind.

RESURGE

Time to remember
Now this year has spelt out
Ultimate syllables
What perhaps nerved it.
Thinking of sheep bells
From the stones of Schiara
And toppling blind drunk
Into a gutter.

Crying for drugs to
Make the pain tolerable;
Then once more serviceable,
My students nurturing
Into the silences
Where all good words tend,
Posthumous violences
Stamped on a world's end.

Horror my brother, nausea my sister
In this year's dark half
Enduring the fissure
Of what had seemed myself;
Hospitalisation,
Then slowly the brightening
Dawn of creation,
The keystone splintering
And novelty, quickness.

DECEMBER

How cold this night is
Of mid-December,
Despite the burning gas
And my pullover.

Almost it could be dawn,
But with no brightening,
I miss the birds' orison
And summer and autumn, but spring
Could not happen without
This dark, this freezing.

It is the condition of light,
As on my year in hospital
Depends the joy I have now
That shivers at light's footfall.

I could not be posthumous
Without a funeral,
Or share a life with a dying
Rinsed with such energy.
It transcends the zest of living;
But I seek my daily bread
And prepare a car for the road.

It would be good if there was
Another word for the name of God.

EXODUS

I remember on my last day in the asylum
On my way to the shop to buy cigarettes
Being accosted by one in madness continuum
And who progressed in that shuffle they have and little leaps.

He gripped me by the throat and announced –
I remember still that grip and my spasm of fear –
'You're dead, you're dead, you're dead',
And then he let go of me and began to caper,

Singing, 'I'm the only man in the world left alive',
Down the corridor he vanished singing,
In the extremis of that solitude lunatics have.

I bought my cigarettes and packed for leaving.

CONVERSATION PIECE

Who did so successfully,
And yet so painfully,
Harrow the darkness?

'Not I,' said the Ego.
'I suffered fission,
Too great for me that stress.'

Then was it the body,
Used to the mountains,
Rockfall and glacier?

'Though abused,' said the body,
'Since I had been well used,
I did my duty, bore what I could bear;
But harrowed hell?
I am no seer!'

Wife, then, friends, brother,
And you, my daughter?

'We saw him taken
By the dark from us.
We did not harrow.'

Then the unconscious,
Though being clinical,
A word that's ephemeral,
That points to the nameless,
Vigilant, vagrant
And is serviceable?

It is what was present,
With everyone absent
In the stifling darkness,
Intelligent integer,
Harrowing darkness,
Harrowing, harrowing.

ALCOHOLISM

It is a sickness of the soul
By no means as yet understood.
To most doctors almost virgin soil,
A ghostliness at the back of the head
Where all the turbid mysteries are
Beginning to shoulder into mind
By the grace of sage and avatar,
One of whom said: 'Seek and you'll find.'

For such findings among the imponderables
In a great darkness I labour now,
Making letters words, words syllables,
Then sentences and paragraphs grow,
Voltaged with quite uncommon sense.

The numinous it is I know
Must come and end marred circumstance,
Let a way of being human die;
I mean marred and conditioned ego,
Then summer wind, both breed and blow
Uncreatured personality.

ZENNOR

Have you, the beautiful
As a Greek medallion,
Letters like mine spell:
Love has no ending,
Though others loving
With complete conviction?

Binding and finding
Cornwall and a morning
Of sunlight and sea-gulls
Nestling and calling
From out of the rock-falls.

For my ring you gave blue
Stones of the amethyst
Ecstasy nerving you
Joy in our new trust.

Then in the evening
By the sea and the wine,
Late swallows swooping,
Your fingers and mine,

Naked we'd hover
Salt in our faces:
How their flanks quiver
Poseidon's horses.

SCHIZOPHRENIA

They cannot be alive in eternity.
They cannot be alive in time.

But are in both places all the same.
I don't know, but I seem to see

A car grinding between two gears,
Unable to get into either

Or screech and grind any louder.
Then a terrible silence follows.

MATURATION

If we were very good at it, it is unlikely we would be human,
Since there would be no need to grow in this now and here;
As it is, we have much to deal with, rage, grief, fear,
Even just the question of loving one man or woman,
Not looking elsewhere

When our partner sees how devious we are under the mask
We wear to disguise the hypocrite, the mask of rectitude,
And yawns at the party story which is their platitude;
Yet growing with one relevant partner is the task,
Not changing when the game strikes home to a new player.

And if we are lucky we do move out and over
Dead selves to what is novel and more serene
And learn from others than ourselves about the scene.
We are intended to go on like this and more discover,
Slowly feeling our way into the infinite harbour.

MY WIFE

It's good you're a sanguine person
With such resilience to pain,
Since life seems to aim and hit you
Again and yet again.

It's not that you do not feel deeply,
It's the very intensity
Of your feelings lets it pass through
Without septicaemia,

And that joy is your natural climate,
And that weather will always return,
After sodden rain and the frost blight
And myself who can blind and burn.

HALLOO

To keep the wolf at bay
And the criminal from the door,
Turn the key, put it in your pocket;
But over the bracken moor
A gang of enormous featureless creatures
Advance from their separate hells,
United in their wish for damages,
You, my love, I and you.

To keep us from the virtuous,
Bent upon any old crime,
To print upon each of us
Features the same as their own.
Assert your individuality
With cunning, but whatever the cost;
To the river to appalling music
Drift regiments of the lost.

For the sake of our predicate –
Nothing but the wish to cancel it out
Is a fitting target for hate –
Listen on far hills the one-eyed monsters shout
From peak to peak hallooing each other
That men and women still have two eyes
Despite their directives
Horribly scrawled in huge letters
In stone circles, on whitewashed walls
That all should be one and in fetters.

Do not enter their hells.

SUPPER

An evening of good communion, Margaret, Kathleen, Julia
And her man, Hein. The house was still
Where the pictures and the figurines are,
And a sense of a tide at the full
Lapping our feet and electric suns
Shining down in benisons
And rinsing us with their orisons
When five different minds were yet as one
In their wish to know and to be known,
To ravel some complexities out
By feeling and by arduous thought.

Could anything be better than this
Togetherness beneath orange stars,
Individual in a synthesis
Of pain and joy in a novelty
Transcending both and neither one
But just the talk and listening,
The anxious ego lost and gone
As the conversation rivered on?

Kathleen, our friend, Margaret my wife,
My daughter, Julia, and her man,
Who can but praise the timeless hours
Seeped up by speech as indeed they were?
Poseidon's sea-born, plunging cars
Cleaving the water of our fears,
Shell-drawn and borne by foaming horses
Attended by triton and sea maid,
Imaged our oceanic exchanges,
The plumbing syllables that were said.

The mystery of the ordinary,
The speech and silence that we keep,
Calm waters under the surface sea
Is where personality takes shape.
I mean tonight a little further
From my present to further self I'd gone,
Such shinings do indeed occur
That one can hone a life upon,
Or the silence of the Helicon.

DAUGHTER

You are what you are
And for my part
Touch my mind
Rinse my heart
With healing water

Who do what you please
My only daughter
Whose fantasies
You translate into
Doing and being

Novelties that show
Patterns of seeing
Not bargained for
By ancient saying,
Like an unguessed door
Suddenly shaping.

So much apoundage
Of flesh of the body
Is an extension
Of the human soul
Discerned by the senses
And that is all.

You have no defences
Are meaningful.

LEGION

What have I to do with thee?

To a god, the demoniac man
Pinpointed by verity
And starting again to be human.
Through his fractured persona gibbered
The parasitical horde
And he muttered and raved and bled
Pierced by the light of the Lord.

They had entered in through the fission
Of his personality
To feast there and wanton and batten
To escape immortality,
But his selfhood from the distance
Returned as a wayfarer.
The ghosts heard him speak from the silence
And began to fury and swear.

But the finger of God was at work
And they fled, half-blind, from that stranger
To rage by themselves in the dark
The death that they could not bear,
While alive not growing to it.
The new man felt the old self enter
His body where the demons had been,
And thirst ending, drank living water,
Wiser than before and more serene,
Hearing joy in heaven, celestial laughter.

COMPANION

Blind Eros made it impossible to see;
I see now and love what I behold:
Your intellect and power that we unrolled
After the compulsions of sexuality
Are lapsed in your way since I've come back home
Into a rapport that is monogamous
And would not live within a haunted house,
Pain her I love, who shares my bed and name,
And with whom a peace I have I never thought
Would come to me, though it's been dearly bought.

Still I have love for the woman I met tonight
And with whom deep seas of passion I once rode,
Her tangible presence the goal of my manhood:
Now friendship has come and with friendship the light
Upon her features in her curtained room
With cider and her books and one great picture
And I listen to her unscroll her nature
And offer my words with a sense of being at home.

She drove me to the station in her car
And when the train came and we said goodbye
Rinsed was I with a strange security;
It was a foretaste of where the eternals are
And there is no marriage or giving in marriage,
But of thought and feeling a coincidence
Within the continuity of a present tense.

I lit a cigarette in the empty carriage
With delight both in what had been and in going home
To her who shares my bed and shares my name.

MY DAUGHTER JULIA

Why should I say that you are not here?
Are you not always present with us?
Almost sitting opposite me in that chair?
There can be admirable hauntings of a house,
Certainly I talk more to you in your absence –
Where are you now? Oh yes, in Amsterdam –
Than with most people with whom I share a presence,
And I should be grateful to you for such silent saying,
It shows the rapport with those who have left us by dying.

One is not all one has been from birth to dying,
But someone behind all such ephemera,
Made by every detail of the living,
Yet different far from such phenomena,
And that goes on past the burial and the burning,
Though it may not be adjusted to the disincarnate,
And so, as is usually the case, all for returning
Into this ante-room of death we all inhabit.

I hope that you, while you are yet mortal,
Pay your debt to the living and expect you will.

INSOMNIA

Such freedom could be
In streets, in bronze acres,
The sweeps of salt sea,
Images, breakers,
And when night's dark footfall
This house passes,
Making invisible
Well-charted places,
Starlight their spaces.

I cannot sleep and
Hear voices accusing,
Feel sharp claws fasten,
Scraping, chastising;
Far off the green hill
In this sodden corner,
But, however, baleful,
I have strength to listen.

Talk then as you will,
Terrible heritage, life will be blest
After your bitter rages.
I shall not nourish them
On my damp ages.
Such joy as they vanish
And up comes dawn light,
Cleansed of phantasma,
The bad tongues inert,
The good ones stronger.

ALL CHANGE

It will happen this way:
Both you and I will be apart, either night or day,
And yet, though apparently distant and far,
Together, in some abiding station, that we share.

Not that, as you've said, you want continuance,
And you won't get it, all will utterly change,
But what if our changes be synonymous?
Then in that change we'd still share a tense.

So let it come, the changing, either soon or late.
You have known so much of my love – and my hate.
You might not be averse to one behind such ephemera,
To whom, as waves the deep sea, changes mere surfaces are.

LENT

I cannot sleep;
Listen to the stillness
Grow taut into dayscape,
As I to the silence
Of my heart
Am learning to listen
And not to do violence
To my life's intention.
The constant saying
Of the murmuring instant,
I am learning to be knowing,
Furthers new detection,
Furthers outgoing.

It's almost four now,
Two hours from dawn only;
Blossom already
Upon the almond bough
Proves the spring ready
To flash green lightning
From such dead embers,
Purple, white, golden,
Of the brief winter.

Today I put bone-meal
To restore and nourish,
Praying that you, love,
Like the roses may flourish
Who my heart in your heart have;
Go first or me follow,
Tiger is spring and
The dart of the swallow.

KNOWING

If ever I've said anything
That is accurate and not ephemeral
And has at least the lineaments of a poem,
It was spoken through me and the art was all in the waiting.
It is not I who speak, not I at all.

Coming into harbour is coming into the open
Reaches at last of the less splenetic sea,
Since it was by the conditioned, land-locked sea I was shaken,
And now we have room for any errant wind:
The pilot is not my business, not him I was.

Sometimes I am surprised at the extent of your knowing,
And wonder if ever I choose the right line
Like your pictures and their accurate ways of saying
The heartbeat of the mountains and the rain,
And though love is synonymous with knowing,
Knowing so much, know how little is known.

DOMINE

If there are words to help, I summon them
From the darkness of this night and the dark in me,
For your sake seek the benison of a charm
To lift the guilt that blurs your destiny,
Sick rose, to rid you of the invisible worm;

Words like the spittle that made a blind man see.
For you must know that you have done no harm
Beyond that native to humanity
And just by being nourished back the warm
Currents of life out of sterility

And made, for at least this wanderer, a strong home
From a promiscuous, vagrant vacancy:
For words to make the ghosts that haunt you calm,
De profundis clamo ad te, domine .

VERNAL

Under thin webs of soil they linger,
Crocus, snowdrop, aconite, celandine
For the hand to relax of winter
And their white, purple and gold to stain
The clenching morning with colour
Like the return of a musical theme
That seems to return rather faster
The further you travel onwards in time.

Even now where I work and labour,
Whitelands College on Putney Hill,
Pear blossom on one tree blooms with ardour
And I wonder what its pale letters really spell
With such daring to brave January's rigour;
Radiant under the sun such early blossoming
When furled in the bud the gloria of each neighbour.
It must smell spring as thirsty animals scent water
That in the pale, unmuscled light its blooms are singing.

I am glad to be alive in this coming of flowers
After the latency of bloom and the scoured trees,
Save for the evergreen, the cold staunches.
How process circles through uncountable centuries!
I wonder how many of these cycles we shall fulfil
As I walk up and down my room where the books are
And do you think *post mortem* will be seasonable?

I feel nostalgia for the mountains of Snowdonia
Now dusk veils this day of sun bypassing winter
And in the gloom lit electric oranges are glowing
And soon in the clarity of night blurred stars will appear;
There are hands behind hands, and they are never failing.

THE PEARL

You may have in the bank a cool million,
Cars two, at least, and of a perfect kind,
But all you'll have is the area you sweat on
Without the serenity of peace of mind.

That only is the pearl worth all the others.
Blake had it in one room clean and bare,
Transcended tycoons, millionaires and ministers
And of the fabric of eternity was aware.

Energy to him was delight eternal
And he created all through his long life
Diagrams of the celestial and infernal,
Trees in their foliage lovely as his wife.

I mention him to show that not in possessions,
Mistresses or successes that are financial
Can there by any hope for an intermission
Of the pain that is the substance of the soul,

Though it evaporates on being conscious of confusion,
More and still more and more of becoming aware,
Till we penetrate the miasma of illusion,
See through the platitudes of need and care.

A SALUTATION

So great the pressure of feeling,
To bear it of more than mere steel
The body you use for this living.
Diamond, no other jewel
Would not blunt and blur at such usage
As you yield to your dailyness.
Being in love is being of interest
And mine in you never grows less.

We have locked up our cottage in Croesor
And the family adjacent to us
Cannot use it for their dogs' bedroom
And make our summer-house their mess.
I make this inconsequent statement
Because from such details the growing is.

And the mountain two hundred miles from us
In your line drawing seems to be here
In the wind blowing round this still house
With my dog asleep by the fire.

You are diamond, my dear, and immortal,
And if that sounds too much like God,
Who else can trace such lines on steel
Or breathe sweetly so near to the dead?

MORITURI (1)

It's a way of living for dying
That we have to undergo,
Premonitions of bearing doomsday,
Vivace, adagio.
To be rid of material till the want
Is I want to know.

Maturation here for the largesse
That in death is as winds blow.
It's for this that here where things are
Out of things we're meant to grow.

Becoming into seeing and knowing
From the grasping's undertow,
Doing changing into being
And to feelings and more so

Than where here, end-stopped by matter,
We're shortened and to and fro
In small parcels from oblivion
Scissored into come and go.

Listen, though, the door is opening
And the novel lightenings show.

UNPREDICTABLE

Dawn shakes out the light from the blackness;
I do not know whether last night I slept or did not sleep,
I certainly spent a long time courting the silence,
But the ideas teeming around kept me awake.

How little we can will what we do here,
Through the small hours I courted oblivion that did not come.
Mind you, though joy is not of our making, it does occur
And the blight down of sorrow is the same.

It is a question of following the process
Of being human and that's impersonal
As the light leavening at dawn the darkness
And sleep is not merely a question of lying still
But of silence that is musical.

There is hope and at least one can tell
That whatever happens must be bearable.

COLLEGE

Tomorrow that, the next day this,
Precision of duties to be done
And I not other than it is
Would have it so to grow upon.
One needs the chores, their dailyness
To nerve the imagination,
As a stream in a steep rocky course
Generates power it could not gain
If the rock strictures it bypass
Meandering through some beaded plain.

I cast away my sense of guilt
While knowing well I erred and err,
Following it to the first blood spilt,
The twilight of the ancestor.
Forgiving myself, I forgive the dead
For their – I do not know – abuse
Of childhood's vulnerability,
As some great boulder checks the run
Of water which still hurries down,
Stronger for having eluded stone.

I forgive myself the intricacies
Of conduct like the twists and turns
Of boulder-ridden mountain streams.
Hissing with light the waters run,
Then underground, no day, no night,
The foreverness of depression,
Damp, black and sour and no daylight;
But a passing through and temporary,
For obedient to geography
By a red-berried rowan tree
Again the stream encounters day.

Then slow, bereft of mountainside,
But with a steady onward thrust,
Deathwards the sere waters glide,
But know I do, not taking on trust,
But real as this writing hand
That death is only to be born
Into our dying where the stream
No longer serves for metaphor,
Since there, Vaughan said, we need no glass,
And know what the travelling was for,
Profit's vacuity and loss.

BEING ALONE

I must not need in the way I now need and am needing,
In a way inapplicable to the virtue of solitude,
In a way that is analogous to fearing,
And it is of being alone that I am afraid.

But we have to be alone when nearing
Dying, or the next stage of going forward is held back.
Blake died in the middle of singing
And Swedenborg saw his landlady needed no money back.

But too much I have the desire to be with you
And for a completeness that must perish like garden snow
And a way of knowing synonymous with certainty.

I have to learn not to want anybody at all.
It is the way of being without that is beautiful
And implies immortality by being mortal.

COMMON SENSE

Waking is food
I wake from sleep
A new zest running
In my blood

The noise of life
And its clamour
To me refreshed
Species glamour

So is sleeping
The soul stuff waking
Wisdom reaping
A crust breaking

So who cannot
Praise all
Between a birth
A funeral
After dying continuance

Nothing but this
Makes common sense.

BLAME

When you accuse me
As the cause of it all,
Your misery,
And no light trouble,
I shrug my shoulders
But don't turn away,
Take my marching orders,
Intending to stay.

For your natural burning
And gaiety
Is the mark by which
I charter the sea
Of my own turmoiling
Troublesome psyche;
Should I blame what is teaching
Myself about me?

Tonight you announced that
You'd live but five years.
I am dubious about that,
Such vitality's yours.
But do know your candle
Will burn to a stub
You'll leave to a grave
As you go to your sea change
And you travelling on
Other vistas. I hope that
With you I am then.

SENEX

Now that my left thigh
Pains me when I walk,
A partial immobility
Constricts my whole body.
I remember my climbing up
Arete, chimney and gully,
Careless of the great drop
That spun under me.

How far then from the care
I now give getting off buses,
Crossing some small ditch or ridge
Now that my age is sixty
And the years are blunting
The body's knife edge.

Richmond Hill sets me panting
Who clambered the Needles,
Of d'Arves in the Dauphiné
From before dawn to
The last jewel of spent day,
Cattle sleeping beneath
As asleep under straw upon hay
We lay, by ravelling water,
Till choughs jerked us out of sleep.

Never again shall I see
Those Needles of gold in the dawn,
But curiosity is perennial.
May it sustain me
Till with death and the words 'All Change',
I shed the details of routine
For vistas of interest
Beyond the circumscribed range,
The platitudes of rest.

O art's archangel, singe
White paper and my quest
Engrave with acid manhood,
With this maybe arthritic hand
A novel schema of words,
Outlining some hints unknown
Into human circumstance.

These are my Needles of d'Arves
Where I cut small nicks of ice
And balanced up grooves of granite.
We have no abiding place
And erosion increases each minute,
But from the loosing and carnal,
This curiosity, this sense
Of what is to be understood
Reaches into a future tense
As those choughs woke me that morning
Into unguessed needles of gold.

What matters is to continue,
The curious do not grow old.

A VISIT

Two women, two boys and two girls
Came to stay with us from Sweden;
Why do I think of amber and pearls
Now they have gone back again
And smell roses in their rooms
And honeysuckle and myrrh?

As if no other terms
Could such strength and grace infer
Those ten harmonious days
Of caritas and its power
Without circumlocution of shadows.
We have lived like people should

But do not in this concrete area,
In a simplicity of fire,
Like that mosaic of Torcello,
For the blest breathable and good,
But foul to the damned far below
Who long for the bloody wood.

NADIR

Being alive now in the nadir of winter
Cold, damp, clammy the texture of the air
And the blood seems to retreat into the heart's centre,
Gaiety is sitting by a warm fire.

It is a question of waiting on a future
When the sun will bring up again the first flowers
And unthaw the liquids of the body,
When they will not needle so, the freezing stars,
And instead of stasis there will be a running of energy.

Mind you, I suppose I am in my days' September,
Late too at sixty-one and steering into the cold.
May my thoughts grow deeper as I grow older,
Taken into myself and firmly held.

For I would be of that company age does not wither,
But ripens into wider vistas of thought,
Going on, as flesh stiffens, into further
Ways by which novelties of being are caught,
And preserve them in language's imperishable amber;

Moving though under the golden eternals
To gain a new idea is to remember
What always has existed like a lake on the fells,
Lapping gently against its margin of granite;
The flesh may decay, but the mind's energies
Move ever onward with unwearied feet,
Being the predicate of the substances.

BRYNHYFRYD (1)

The day after tomorrow we go to our mountain cottage
By the Cnicht and the Moel Wnion
And not far from the sea's glittering page,
The unskinned stars shining down upon us,
The unsleeping stream among its moss and boulder,

And though slightly crippled with more relish
Affirm the phenomena now that I am older
That not a bird, beast, man will ever perish.
The breathing silence punctuated by night with nothing
And by day by dogs, cropping sheep, the raven,
Far from a city and its bypassing
By noise and interjection, hell and heaven.

If you are strong enough we shall walk down to Porthmoina,
The deserted village and a port when they mined slate,
Where now of a beauty, though few people occur,
Sea and pier and rock all consummate,
I mean the numinous is the landscape.

Little trout filter through their gills the agile water
Of a stream that forks from a precipice near a deserted mine.
I cannot find adequate words for this place here,
But the orange harvest moon may be a sign.

RETIREMENT

Because after thirty years
Paid teaching work comes to a stop,
The notion of ending it jars,
The sense of routine given up
Is a sort of minority of death
As what one was good at disappears.

At least one stage of life is ending,
Going down beneath the years,
Not knowing what next will be beginning,
But knowing the fact that one fears.

It is a failure of nerve, the resources never end
Of the living, and, too, of the dying.
There is never any last stand,
But a continuity of moving
Onwards and ever into
Life evergreen, ever growing,
The death into which we must go.

Since there is no end to becoming:
Half-blind, help me to see
Perpetuity.

FOR MARGARET

I often wonder about identity.
Why it should be this one and not another
With whom one keeps particular company
And how words always seem intended to go further
With this especial someone known so well;

And because of this realise how very far
Short one falls of knowing, while some superficial
Acquaintance after a meeting or two seems well defined
While for the particular one it is never quite that at all.

It is also the sense I have with you of permanence,
Though I know you can be removed by a skidding car,
As if one had reached into irrefrangible essence,
Indifferent to cardiac failure or the erosion of cancer.

And I see no reason to doubt that what I believe,
Because it is comforting, must be a phantasma;
It still eludes Freud's *Future of an Illusion,*
And may be as real as this finger or this chair.

Having experienced with you 'psychic phenomena'
And found it both inexplicable and ordinary,
I see no reason why anything should not occur
Or that a meeting is impossible after we die.

I wonder what would happen if you or I died.
It seems to me, now, you would be irreplaceable
And that life with anyone else would be quite unshared,
Not that I find solitude very tolerable.

Your pictures, though, they have soaked into the walls,
And anyone else's head on your pillow
Would be breaking what we have made, intangible spells
Stronger than life; no one else could follow.

So I sincerely hope you will live and much longer,
Though this metre, dear, is unsuitable for such saying,
This is my way of saying it could not be stronger,
My sense of knowing you, and of loving.

CASA MONTINI

By the patio of the Casa Montini
Look below, the Piave shines
In the dusk where little bats fly
Flickering through the trellised vines.

There we sat together, still,
As the night from evening grew
Like a cup you slowly fill.
A new moon behind Schiara lofted in the ebony blue,
Owls and stars began to hoot and glow.

Wafting from remote Civetta,
Summer night, adagio.

HOME

Back once more in Putney
From Wales and its mountains,
With the books in my study,
The small flowering gardens,
The night-long noises.

I miss the night sky
And the questions of silence
As to living and dying
Which the peopled roads repress,
The launderette bypasses,
Not the field with its horses.

I could not learn dying
Among taxis and buses,
Its colour, its ardour
Of being, of seeing
A musical order,
Here where the great oranges
Lighten our darkness
And tapping heels shatter
The wind of no grasses
And from low walls chatter
Girls with bronze faces.

I tell, I do lecture
Of angel and spectre
In the hope that what is heard
May suggest the mountain
From my cottage window,
Make my students more certain
Of the curtain of shadow,
Of the blood-clotted curtain,
The marshlight of dogma.

CLINICAL DEPRESSION

If it should come again,
One day I wake to the same stunning pain
That black out time and weather
And I know that pain is and nothing further;

Even then it would not be as it was before,
Since never experience is quite similar,
I would know, given dedicated silence,
The greatest storm does yet exhaust its violence.

And I would not as before blur it with alcohol,
But where the lightning and the rain strike let it fall,
Knowing that at times it is my lot to be with the unblessed dead;
If it comes again, I shall but bend my head.

MOUNTAIN

Now that a spinal injury
Has made it impossible to go
Climbing on rock and ice and snow,
I dream of climbing frequently.

Last night, for instance, on firm chalk,
Half free climbing, half on an iron way,
I lofted in aerial ecstasy,
Though capable only of fell walk.

I think that climbing is a metaphor,
The most adequate that here there is
For the way we move from time to the eternities
And that's what all the veridical dreams are for:

To show just how movement is when we are dead,
I mean with an uncircumscribed freedom
In that meaningful and adjacent kingdom
Which by the climbing of rock is suggested.

Botterills Slab, the great gully of the Crag of Craving,
These I sort out today from many another
To celebrate the tincture and odour climbs are
In a moment that is like unsingeing burning.

By this, as by night in dreams,
I constantly follow the perpetual and aerial rockways.
How can it be that I am not learning to praise
The motion towards dying that just now seems

Like a closeness more life into itself gathering
In the last decade or so of my being now here?
The translation into literate dying drawing near
I think of my last climb, Schiara, Golden Ring.

SORROW

I too long have been much frightened
By the sadness of the heart.

Now I know depression is living
And what makes the poems start,
Demon of my outward going,
I am nourished by my hurt,
Take him for my friend
From whom never again shall I be apart,

Though I winced and wriggled from him
In the arms of riot,
Sluiced down alcohol to avoid
The great verities of quiet,
Rather than encounter sadness
Sought the gutter and the dirt.

Friend, now I with joy salute you,
Neither terrified nor curt,
On my sixty-first year of being human
In the speech of art,
Arm in arm with joy, with sorrow
Find the company I sought.

CRIB-Y-DYSGIL

Once more and by Crib-y-Dysgil,
Snowdon, I would climb again,
That's the sheer side. It's no banal
Track chattering and human.
No, it is the stream which babbles
Working down through stone and grass
Underneath my youth-climbed gullies
Of the mountain of Cwm Glas,
Past Bochwyd's well-loved buttress
Diamonded with streaks of quartz.

Now at sixty such the climbs were
Of my youth I don't regret
(Past my skill and strength they now are),
Since not one I can forget,
And there is a new-found pleasure
In the time for looking I've gained
At the cirrus crossing azure
Skyscapes, rushes in the wind,
And that buzzard hanging over
Its next meal above the coomb,
Rabbit warrened, near the shadow
Of Cwm Glas's ebony stone,
On whose Central Wall I balanced
Almost three decades ago,
Enjoying safe moves, quite unchanced,
And the precipice below.

It just makes the intimacy greater
Now I labour under the walls,
Noting the crag's shaped like a mitre;
Day springs flow from different wells,
Nothing goes if you are ready
To take the offering,
Like that hawk balanced so steady
On the bronze of each delicate wing.

I am glad of a visionary eye
And the novelty of each morning.
May it be so till the cord break
And looses me into dying,
Even more, and more broad awake:
Meanwhile I think of Crib-y-Dysgil
By its suitable ease unperplexed.
Can't you see that we live a serial,
Are continued in our next?

HEADLINED REVIEW

It's good the way the working's coming out,
It's personal still but steadily outreaching
To a small coterie no longer bound
But in strange hearts and minds and nerve ends meeting.

The inwardness shouldering up, the pen, the print
Reaching strange glands by syllables of cord,
After so many hours of doing my stint,
To other nervous systems the arrow of the Word.

And critics starting to speak at last like this one
On my desk tonight involved in mind and heart
With the books and energies I have worked on
For three decades, it was time for the talking to start.

However, I offer laudations to the quiet,
Since dying to each day's sameness is what I am at,
A dying in which the words may walk abroad
And that's what all my poems are about.

JUBILATE

This stranger that joy is
All I know it has come
With its intensities
To the heart home;
After the melancholia
Which held sway for decades
Apassionata
Clashing sword-blades
In a high, keen rhythm
The dancer parades
To the beat of a drum
Out of the shades
To where sunlight is
Foaming in the sky
After declivities
The wishing to die,
Such abysses of
Drugged apathy.
Now birds of morning
Shake sleep from their eyes
As the last star fades
Untiring and wise:
That from such experience
Of the soul's dark night
Comes novel joy and sense
Shakes me with light.

THERE

Where the flowers are, where the birds are, water for them, bits of
bread
In our garden where the roses grow serene, unblemished,
Purple aubrietia on the rockery, clumps of it and widely spread
And a poisonous laburnum hangs down low its golden head:

Images of the more brilliant colours we shall know when we are
dead.
Flowers, when we learn to see them, far more golden, purple, red,
Than the vegetable copies which down here are nourished,
Far less brilliant than in the condition of our dying are stated,

Where to feel's to speak though no specific language is stated
And since we see without a dark glass can't be misinterpreted,
Where no subterfuge is possible so we can't be cheated,
Ego and its complex confusions of bad chance at last being shed,
Who would not unhinge material for the freedom of the dead?

Peonies are in our front garden scarlet and infoliated,
Twenty of them from death's kingdom accurately copied
And the white enamoured roses by the sunlight unfurled,
Crackling fire about the body and you're free at last instead
Of the need for the unquiet, and your breath and daily bread.

LAUDATE

White light on the Moel Wnion
Where still in April the sun
Glistens as if it were winter
Though the daffodils gleam and glow
And under the snow the heather
Is greening for sunshine and May.
I see it all in my mind's eye
Though I am far away.

For mice and small birds a buzzard
Is hawking it over the hills;
Shall I, with a cracked lumbar,
Read what Moel Wnion spells?
Where a great rock-face like a profile
Stretches from scree to heather –
'It must be more than a mile' –
I shall know in the coming summer
Whether I lose or fail,

But whether it's loss or failure,
Life is a blessing to me,
Ravens tumble round Snowdon,
Oyster-catchers interpret the sea
And whatever the next page turns over
I shall see the mountain called Cnicht
Glittering in the morning, powdered by stars at night.

MOEL WNION

Away from me in Wales the sheep are grazing
Above my cottage on a soaked mountain.
I hear the steady beat of their crunching
And see on wool the sparkle of the spring rain,
The clouds' life over the Moel Wnion.
Interpret I can the words of the wind
Brushing the grasses, it affirms no oblivion,
No death, no beginning and no world to end
And I know then or when I watch the peeled stars
Something of the language of this valley and a part
Of its dialogue between dreaming and waking
Between the unskinned mind and the fractured heart.

There are dark places upon the Moel Wnion,
The shale hole for copper with a sheep's skeleton,
Crevasses for metal, in rock-faces blasted
Where the ferns at the dripping edges turn towards the sun
Away from – one thinks of Kurtz's 'The horror! The horror!';
Have I not also from sorrow and mania turned away?
But the time has come to confront the origin of error
And pay the price I am supposed to pay.

THE RAVEN

In asterisks of morning
My sleep-soaked body
Is avid for doing,
The day to study,
Plumed like a raven,
Hauled by the updraught,
Its wings wide open
Tumbling in the wind-shaft
Of the plumed morning.

I cannot now climb
The cliffs of Snowdon,
Sixty years brought that stop.
As for morning walking
I shall know by Easter
How effective my going
With a chipped lumbar.

But still there'll be mountains,
The raven of morning,
Despite the year's stains
Which are death's premonition,
And I sense freer going
From that intermission
And wider knowing
With the vegetable, carnal
World changed to spirit
In every good detail,
Ours to inherit.

Never shall being fail.
There is no end to it.

POSTHUMOUS

Walking, the beautiful men and women
Are printed in time till their time runs away
And they go into an accustomed novelty
With which strangely they are strangely familiar.

Even now when they are wonderful
More shall they be in their ecstasy
Of transformation where it is possible to see
With no dark glass and so more meaningfully,

As they come out of time into the transfiguration,
Into their beauty and where they are most serene
With never any detritus to come between
Their capacity for the fullest communion.

As those who are young and beautiful,
So shall it be with those who are lined and old,
Backwards their temporal being is unrolled,
Till like the moon they are and at the full.

It is only passing from one room to another
And that has been happening always and is not remarkable,
Though of infernos the silly stories tell.
All shall be well except those rooted in matter

Who return here for another session in the material
In the hope of at last seeing as it is
The ephemera of being as half-fantasies,
Till they comprehend life's story is not all.

But for the beautiful and serene, there is no returning,
Who die in death as they died in their lives,
Like an undulation of sea-waves,
An unsingeing and unwithering forever of burning.

PATHWAYS

The heron haunted
Curlew chanted
Feathered lake of
Craig-y-Adern
Fed by the water
Whose gabble, whose whisper
From the mountain of Knight
Comes tumbling down.

We shall be there when
July is well in
And an excess of leafage
That seems evergreen
From our window looking upon the mountain
That whatever the weather
Can but remain.

The evergreen instant
Caught by the eternal
Is always present.
I shall climb through the rock-fall
Of the lake to the ridge that
Leads on to the Knight
And labour up it
To the cairn on the summit.

MORITURI (2)

There is great moonlight, but I see no moon,
Only the evidence of whitened trees and houses.
It must be shadowed by some slight cloud's stain;
I feel like this about someone who dies;
That though death suffuses a kind of glow
Real as the moonlight or last evening's rain,
The sense of their not being mortal does not show,
Despite some evidence that they carry on,
Not show except as a kind of whitening
Muffled by a cloudburst of opacity;
Perhaps it's because we want so much clear seeing
That what might be certain is uncertainty.

I mean by striving to come too close we cannot see
More than the tombstone letters we figure out,
So that what should at least be a vacuity
And not so much like a stone slab as a gate
Not into, perhaps, a second mortality,
But what we hate to mention, I mean death.
Hate, since we find it hard to bear uncertainty.
Look now, the moon has surfaced from that cloud
And has never for one moment ceased to be,
Though last night in the rain no light was shed,
It now grains every stone and shining tree.

Blake said: 'The body is that portion of the soul
Discerned – in time and space – by the five senses';
And if that's true, it doesn't matter at all
If with its minor part the soul dispenses.
Soon into blackness I'll stare on the brink of sleep.
We die, you know, each night and dreams suggest
Distances travelled despite our prone, still shape.
Of course one knows sleep's only an interval;
But shouldn't it also be a metaphor
Of the fact that at last ripeness will be really all,
Although quite other growings may occur?

Dogs bark from the nearby, sleeping farms
And mine, though half asleep, seems to murmur.
God, how I hate that stuff about the worms
And skulls and ashes, dung and mummia!
It's been going on as long as life, this dying,
And familiarity should have made us grow more fond
And so enhance its twin, the joy of living.
Let's show some unworried zest for our temporal end.
Vaughan said: 'They have all gone into the world of light' –
And he was a man who meant just what he said.
The moon has now gone under a heavy cloud;
The stones, the trees, the mountains are quite dead.

DUALITIES

Most remarkable is
The Word made flesh, intensities
Where the growing seems to fit
Discordancies of flesh and spirit

Which nourish for further far
Growings where the immortals are,
Using for learning, mortality,
Nourishing what must be,

That we may learn here
In print which is small
How to read more clear
The eternal
And be there more at home
By the narrowness of our aim.

Patience, *patio*, I suffer, is
More at home there, for what here was.
This is the mechanics of the Word
Made flesh. My first dying occurred
On a Monday in July.

Now I perish perpetually
In the old man to renew
A vision always going askew,
Seeing clearly I shall go far
Distances where the immortals are.

STEEL

I have discarded opiates of despair,
The drugged furore aurora that was killing me
As I staggered, soused, to an indifferent bed
And now stare astounded at the birds in the sky.

For the unparagraphed exists I thought I never should know,
Blurring my capacities to think and feel.
Now I feel on my face the stinging north wind blow,
Time, petal by petal, unfolds a rose of steel.

SOBER

The galaxies of revolving sphere
Cool gently a blond summer air.
I sense the chemicals leaving my blood
And suffer less by choosing to suffer.

Five fabulous lions my senses are,
Swinging back to cool in natural
Rhythms that labour to occur
Not singed by ivy, alcohol.

The bitter gulpings vapour far
In iced and boreal arctic seas.
Who would have thought such clemencies
After brandy and the bar?

The shakings and the strangled breath,
The search for a centimetre of drink,
Tumbler by tumbler each a death,
Life in a suffocating chink.

The valediction of the rose
Where only ghosts can breed and blow
In the balefire of a beaten cause
The appalling whimper of the snow.

DAUPHINÉ

Aiguille d'Arves, that's where we two climbed
More than three decades ago,
With an impulse shared by one mind
To unravel rock and snow,
Needles threading the sky and golden
And the sheep-bells far below.

Now time's solvent has dissolved my
Zest for climbing, memories
Of our expeditions together
Fasten on my earth-bound days.
In my chair I sit and wonder
At the word my past time says
Of those nicks I cut in thin ice
And the rocks as histories.

Beating at midday in silence
To the final tower of all
Where we solved with skill, and good sense
Problems that were vertical,
Reached the climb's last circumstance.
Then, roped, down through the immense
Airy nothing over all,
So it seemed, afternoon and France,
To the hut below the snow-line.

From my chair it's no distance.

NOBIS PACEM

It is only now in my sixth decade that instead of
Trying to live life, I let life live me.
Why it should be so and so belatedly
I'm not sure, though it has something to do with love.

What I mean to say is enjoying myself and others in no half-
Way house, but simply by letting life grow through me,
Using my faculties for what is intended for the creature
By that more than I who is my friend and creator.

Until this year forcing life into my pattern of living,
I lived in a parody: sex, mountains, alcohol,
Not realising as I fled, being a depressive, the latter is a depressant.
Dullness was my twin and all but the hepped-up moment intolerably
dull.

I am, as Blake said, the secretary of the word,
And to get words down with an extreme accuracy
Have ravaged myself almost to excess and with brutality.
Lighten our darkness, for we tend to live in the half-dark.

Growing to love, the poetry at last wafts over to my neighbour.
I mean what I wrote with the writing the only reward
Is at last beginning to be understood
And after three decades of deliberate labour.

It is not in status or being the poet that the joy is,
But talking to others in good communions,
And being lived by the life that is brighter than a thousand suns.
It is becoming the self that forever was.

I think, as Blake said, that dying is passing from one room to
another.
Having explored my dying and found in it no terror,
It is a question of being blessed and learning to bless.

Note: A version of this poem under the titler 'Pax' was included in *Bread for the
Winter Birds*. I include the present one as the better of the two. Professor Sharrock
has pointed out that *nobis pacem* are the last two words of the Agnus Dei in the
Latin Eucharist: *Agnus Dei, qui tollis peccata mundi: dona nobis pacem.* – J.M.

MEETING

These people round me are the books I read,
Who used to read books people to escape,
At least in part, being frightened of my need
For good communion and companionship.

Now in some aspects of myself more wise,
Though goodness knows I've far, far, far to go,
I look my neighbour straightly in the eyes
And read the word he says or dare not say,

And doing so find that I find myself
In the meeting with a man or with a woman,
Whether it's a question of hatred or of love
Or some mixed gradation between them that's more common.

I also find the origin we're children of,
The intricate predicate of mortality
That when we're no longer of this flesh and mortal
With unbandaged eyes, I shall learn how to see.

SPEED

You need not go far to go further
Than those who tick up mileage in a car.
You can circumvent the world in your chair
And trace the deeps and the moon where the great deadnesses are.

The faster you move, your stay is the stiller.
It is a question of knowing what occurs and does occur.
The quest is not reckoned by the speedometer
Where distances are registered which go from nowhere to nowhere.

I shall stay here, I shall not go to the Sahara,
Nor, to my regret, ever see the Himalaya,
But say that I have gone very far,
For it is, and without a mirror,
Or turning to stone, confronting the Medusa,
Her green eyes, the snakes in her wet hair.

By that image I become more
Than what I attempted, that is to ignore
It is a questioning of the welcoming stare,
Until what caused the pain is no longer quite there.

Speed is not going fast that can reach nowhere.
Maybe in a chair it is becoming more aware
Of the monster and the horn at the centre.
I see four men loose walking in the fire.

Note: The last line refers to Daniel 3: 25. The three were Shadrach, Mesbach and
Abednego. The verse reads: ' . . . Lo, I see four men loose, walking in the midst of
the fire, and they have no hurt; and the form of the fourth is like the Son of God.'
Blackburn published a book of verse with the title *The Fourth Man* in 1971. – J.M.

AGEING

It is strange, this stiffening of the flesh and muscle with later age,
For the mind's as quick as ever in the hardening of its cage.
Once each, every impulse followed to my wishing and my need
And the zest of wind and mountain accompanied my ardent speed.
I remember coursing down from Idwall light and feathered as my
                                                              need
To celebrate the zest of movement, aerial nothingness my food
Racing through the turf and boulders, light with joy and impersonal
From my rock climbing on Cwm Idwall,
Such surplusage of energy.

Now my running and climbing are for the most part from my chair.
The mind must quicken for the body,
Or hardening sinews and despair,
Range the further and the lighter as the flesh gets heavier.
Watch, too, with more accurate looking
Now that doing's more difficult
How the liquid to a streamlet from a barricade is spilt,
Green and ochre as if marble, cool and many-coloured
Columns of falling water built,
Or a cloudscape lit by wanlight from the thin and vernal sun
Smouldering over a new greenness just emerging from the dun
Heather and bracken of the winter now that springtime has begun.

But the mind and spirit must quicken
As the body ceases to be
The equivalent of the heart's zest
Or a dead urbanity.
I must range from my book-lined study
Infinite mileages of thought
Or be trapped within the dead end of a stale identity,
Perish contours of oblivion,
Somnolent, sexagenarian, foreshortened, stiff;
Though in one room I must journey,
I must learn, travelling to dying, at my destiny to laugh,
And then bodiless in dominion
Motion will be as the far-reaching thought:

No more in this carnal enclave;
Astral, numinous and taut.

MID-OCTOBER

Fears for far
Distances, the destinies of most of us here are,
As they are corroded by travelled instances,
Our abodes in a contracting now, the substances
We walk and speak in which passing time turns over
To a cold, crabbed side in which it is hard to discover
The lineaments, in youth plain, of the spirit
Which remains inward though the crunched outside does not show it.

I watch them pass in the spring and summer
Of a carnality which shows clear
Through the scarlet mouth, the nostril, eyes, their glittering
Supernormal energies travelling
In a breathing-space where they occur,
The darker incidents in which the feelings are.

Passing time scars lines in the carnal,
Which, if drawn right, also shows the eternal;
It depends whether we have been able to continue
To keep ourselves open for the wind to blow through,
Or hardened, fearing to feel, into a platitude
Which says only what is not worth being said.
But never ever, though living not to live we may try,
Are we not in living and dying what is and consciously.

For a novel beauty the decades are intended for.
What counts is being each changing phase without nostalgia,
As they go in their carnal flame to affirm passing,
Though soaked ours must be, if it is, in further knowing.
I celebrate, may it be humility, the creature
In a becoming which is synonymous with forever,
The now of it which cannot fail to occur,
Since it is immortal and where the immortals·are.

TO BE CONTINUED

Now in this temporal, intermediary, colloquial
Interregnum of being, brief meeting, short saying,
Where mercenary doing seems the being and end all,
I have lived before birth is, I have lived after dying
And gathered in meaning in sheaves by the armful.

Though quite out of tune with the material stuff here
I admit it's needed or I should not be living;
It is hell, perhaps, the dominion of life where the lives are
Labouring for death and a different meaning.

So better before it, the heart stop, the choking, catches us napping,
To admit to our programme the apparent full stop,
Since it's really a comma, a further ushering,
A new way where old customs at last drop
And imagination is the essential

Condition, not getting the new house, the new car,
But feeling, thinking, feeling remote from such objects,
Difficult for some of us, serenely to bear,
To live without graspable, perishable subjects,
The communion of death, its sparser habits.

I don't want to come again where the dominion of life is,
To have, hold and digest world with no end,
Where all is timetabled, financial, synthesis.
Help me, you numinous self of my self, to defend
This black-capped stage, particular being.

NEVER THE LESS

Never the less, love, seems my loving but if anything more so
As between the spaces of living with you now I come and go
Like the water of a river hithering ever to and fro
As between the Cnicht, our mountain, salted winds forever blow.

I've been thinking, we've been reading Virginia Woolf's biography.
Loved and rich and justly famous her books enlarge the sympathy
And her beautiful classic features and her wit and gaiety,
Yet she chose, under wings of madness, to blot out her identity;

With a great stone in her pocket walked into the water and
Sought beyond the suffocation for a peaceful state of mind
Here in time and place though honoured and befriended she couldn't
                                                                find,
Chose the dying she'd not reckoned with, teetered out and took its hand.

Such a multitude of occasions for bewilderment there are;
Pose us where the furious traffic though extant seems not to stir,
Where the fractured present moment transcends itself, becomes entire,

And the immediacies of present seep back to the eternal,
As far out in midnight waters, steady clanging, a sea-bell
Undoes notions and moment as by right and funeral
Yet forever Eastering clamour. What's the right word? Who can tell?

PRE-NATAL

I have been to where I was before I was born
And in quiet dialogue the self and I
Decided upon my birthplace, a sufficiency
Of evil in it and the child was to be torn
By forces which, though terrible, I indeed
Chose for my multifarious purposes.
It was more terrible to read the sentences
In that black script and its wanton hammer-blows,
And there, with the man I had chosen to call Father,
To travel faster and much further.

For by subjecting me to his crooked regimen,
Directing against me all that could abuse the soul,
He speeded the process by which I could become serene and whole
And in doing so succour dead women and dead men.
For four decades he has been to me anathema,
But though I castigate him in red letters,
It was I myself who chose the thumbscrew and the fetters;
For it was myself decided to go down there.

And he did what he did because of his conditioning,
Though what he did was perverse *in extremis*,
It was done with the best of intentions, nothing amiss,
So that now, more detached, I behold the happenings
And know that only by forgiveness can I exorcise
The image of the idiot he fastened on me,
Can but know I am solicited for sympathy.
How could he help the astigmatism of his dreadful eyes?

To become whole I slough off the conception of incubus;
Forgive us our trespasses as we forgive those who trespass against us.

CHOOSING

I choose to be here and with that family,
Coming with the self before I was born.
'You will go down there, vulnerable to your enemy?'
'Yes, I shall go. It is the place where I can learn.'

So I went down and endured the tyranny,
The spinning madness of my own flesh father,
But realised it was I, now in my sixty-first year,
Who had chosen him to become the maker.

And knew myself before the origin
Talking with love and confidence to the more than I
About just how the place of meeting did begin
And that we'd met before congealed entity.

Since I myself had chosen to endure just this birth,
How can I blame them that it is difficult,
To the child I was abuse and bald insult,
For life complexities I needed their living death
And that I wrestled with half-blind at Ephesus.

Forgiving enemies the conclusion is
And the love of children whose sour destinies
Have not quenched that they are the blessed children of God.

BRYNHYFRYD (2)

I really should not sit up quite so late
Upon white paper talking to myself,
And trying to make the rhymes and words come right
And so some portion of those problems solve
Which like sea-waves break on my shore of mind
And leave a little to be interpreted
Within a murmuration of new sound.

Sometimes I seem to be talking with the dead,
Here in this cottage on the fells for instance
Where many men and women have lived and died,
Leaving down here some troubled circumstance
Which maybe would help them if it could be solved.
Is that what probing myself I'm trying to do,
Since by an understanding they may understand
And by that, into further living, die?
They seem so close on this sheep-grazing ground.

I cannot talk about eternity,
Death's synonym, for being finite and human,
The hollow sound bypasses what we can say
Who only know that death is surely coming,
It is perhaps our only certainty.
The kettle on the stove is slowly humming
And soon I'll make myself some fresh coffee,
Not knowing what trap is waiting to be sprung,
But conscious by bird-song of approaching day.

The wind is blowing inwards from the heath,
I hope it blows this quenching mist away.
My wife said that she found it hard to breathe
And when she cannot breathe what shall I do?
How it returns the vacuity of death
And does it end words by approaching you?

I want to live not caring if I die
And so more certain of a strong wish to live;
It's time now to drink up my black coffee,
And know that no one lies within a grave,
But changes in the 'twinkling of an eye'.
For lack of other words those words will serve
Better than murmurs of eternity.

I often think though that the words we have
Echo and outwards and to those who are dead;
How difficult it is to come near to love,
Though it's high time the word was firmly banished.
Maybe the language is reciprocal
And from it comes what we never thought before.
I know 'unconscious' is more usual,
But that word's really a label, nothing more,
And only means what its dead letters spell;

Dead once again. Never more fixed in living
Have I ever been before at any time,
As if beyond my capacity for believing
Some archer using me took steady aim,
And although I am not certain of his target
I take great pleasure in the arrow's flight.

WITH YOU

The thought my mind will not steady on
Is my looking into the muzzle of a gun:
You gone,
My home falling down.

Not that I believe in absence,
But the gap of your immediate lost presence
Would to communion do irreparable violence;
Not that it will be so,
I sense there is a long time for us to go.
We have just moved into joy from sorrow.

I can be with you without speaking
And it is more satisfying than most speech,
And it is only with you that I have known the meaning of touching
And it is far beyond the circumstances of touch.

Some demonic forces we have endured together!

I speak of paranoia now that the paranoia has gone,
But there were stretches of Amazonian and polar weather
It was your destiny to endure alone,
Since my speech was the antithesis of silence,
An amalgam of lunacy and violence.

Now at sixty-one I come into the calm weather
That has always been the climate in which you move
And we realise the pities together
And what it is further understanding to have.

But it is the ordinariness of communion I enjoy,
Sitting silent and then the word not too idle,
As it was in our flowering garden yesterday,
For you see it is all a myth, all a fable.

PURGATORIAL

Tonight through the leafage of a tree a single star.
I saw it with eyes unskinned as perhaps it is,
A mineral diagram of the numinous
Glittering down from where the eternals are.

It was an image of what I had written today,
Of Dante supported by Virgil fainting through
The excrement of Satan and his crew,
Then rock, a star, the purgatorial way.

I also have my Virgil and my words
And travelled recently a similar road
Through my own dung and claustrophobic blood,
Then faint, a star, a symphony of birds.

The carnal is congealed ghost but the stress
Of being carnal need not be too great.
Though over sixty it is not too late
To learn, constant in blessing, how to bless.